BASEBALL LEGENDS

Hank Aaron
Grover Cleveland Alexander
Ernie Banks
Johnny Bench
Yogi Berra
Roy Campanella
Roberto Clemente
Ty Cobb
Dizzy Dean
Joe DiMaggio
Bob Feller
Jimmie Foxx
Lou Gehrig
Bob Gibson
Rogers Hornsby
Reggie Jackson
Shoeless Joe Jackson
Walter Johnson
Sandy Koufax
Mickey Mantle
Christy Mathewson
Willie Mays
Stan Musial
Satchel Paige
Brooks Robinson
Frank Robinson
Jackie Robinson
Pete Rose
Babe Ruth
Nolan Ryan
Mike Schmidt
Tom Seaver
Duke Snider
Warren Spahn
Willie Stargell
Casey Stengel
Honus Wagner
Ted Williams
Carl Yastrzemski
Cy Young

NEWFIELD
PUBLICATIONS

BASEBALL LEGENDS

WARREN SPAHN

Peter C. Bjarkman

Introduction by
Jim Murray

Senior Consultant
Earl Weaver

CHELSEA HOUSE PUBLISHERS

New York • Philadelphia

Published by arrangement
with Chelsea House Publishers.
Newfield Publications and design
are federally registered trademarks
of Newfield Publications, Inc.

CHELSEA HOUSE PUBLISHERS

Editorial Director: Richard Rennert
Executive Managing Editor: Karyn Gullen Browne
Copy Chief: Robin James
Picture Editor: Adrian G. Allen
Art Director: Robert Mitchell
Manufacturing Director: Gerald Levine

Baseball Legends
Senior Editor: Philip Koslow

Staff for WARREN SPAHN
Copy Editor: Catherine Iannone
Editorial Assistant: Scott Briggs
Designer: M. Cambraia Magalhães
Picture Researcher: Alan Gottlieb
Cover Illustration: Daniel O'Leary

Library of Congress Cataloging-in-Publication Data

Bjarkman, Peter C.
   Warren Spahn/Peter C. Bjarkman: introd. by Jim Murray.
      p. cm. — (Baseball legends)
   Includes bibliographical references (p.   ) and index.
   Summary: A biography of the major league pitcher who holds the
record for the most wins by a southpaw.
   ISBN 0-7910-1191-7. — ISBN 0-7910-1225-5 (pbk.)
   1. Spahn, Warren. 1921-   — Juvenile literature. 2. Baseball
players — United States — Biography— Juvenile literature. 3. Pitchers
(Baseball) — United States — Biography — Juvenile literature.
[1. Spahn, Warren, 1921-   . 2. Baseball players.]   I. Title.
II. Series.
GV865.S6B53   1992
796.357´092 — dc20   91-228897
[B]   CIP
                                                                     AC

CONTENTS

WHAT MAKES A STAR

Jim Murray

No one has ever been able to explain to me the mysterious alchemy that makes one man a .350 hitter and another player, more or less identical in physical makeup, hard put to hit .200. You look at an Al Kaline, who played with the Detroit Tigers from 1953 to 1974. He was pale, stringy, almost poetic-looking. He always seemed to be struggling against a bad case of mononucleosis. But with a bat in his hands, he was King Kong. During his career, he hit 399 home runs, rapped out 3,007 hits, and compiled a .297 batting average.

Form isn't the reason. The first time anybody saw Roberto Clemente step into the batter's box for the Pittsburgh Pirates, the best guess was that Clemente would be back in Double A ball in a week. He had one foot in the bucket and held his bat at an awkward angle—he looked as though he couldn't hit an outside pitch. A lot of other ballplayers may have had a better-looking stance. Yet they never led the National League in hitting in four different years, the way Clemente did.

Not every ballplayer is born with the ability to hit a curveball. Nor is exceptional hand-eye coordination the key to heavy hitting. Big-league locker rooms are filled with players who have all the attributes, save one: discipline. Every baseball man can tell you a story about a pitcher who throws a ball faster than anyone has ever seen but who has no control on or *off* the field.

The Hall of Fame is full of people who transformed themselves into great ballplayers by working at the sport, by studying the game, and making sacrifices. They're overachievers—and winners. If you want to find them, just watch the World Series. Or simply read about New York Yankee great Lou Gehrig; Ted Williams, "the Splendid Splinter" of the Boston Red Sox; or the Dodgers' strikeout king Sandy Koufax.

A pitcher *should* be able to win a lot of ballgames with a 98-miles-per-hour fastball. But what about the pitcher who wins 20 games a year with a fastball so slow that you can catch it with your teeth? Bob Feller of the Cleveland Indians got into the Hall of Fame with a blazing fastball that glowed in the dark. National League star Grover Cleveland Alexander got there with a pitch that took considerably longer to reach the plate; but when it did arrive, the pitch was exactly where Alexander wanted it to be—and the last place the batter expected it to be.

There are probably more players with exceptional ability who didn't make it to the major leagues than there are who did. A number of great hitters, bored with fielding practice, had to be dropped from their team because their home-run production didn't make up for their lapses in the field. And then there are players like Brooks Robinson of the Baltimore Orioles, who made himself into a human vacuum cleaner at third base because he knew that working hard to become an expert fielder would win him a job in the big leagues.

A star is not something that flashes through the sky. That's a comet. Or a meteor. A star is something you can steer ships by. It stays in place and gives off a steady glow; it is fixed, permanent. A star works at being a star.

And that's how you tell a star in baseball. He shows up night after night and takes pride in how brightly he shines. He's Willie Mays running so hard his hat keeps falling off; Ty Cobb sliding to stretch a single into a double; Lou Gehrig, after being fooled in his first two at-bats, belting the next pitch off the light tower because he's taken the time to study the pitcher. Stars never take themselves for granted. That's why they're stars.

THE BRIDGE AT REMAGEN

In March 1945, 24-year-old Warren Spahn, a lanky staff sergeant in the 276th Engineer Combat Battalion ofthe U.S. Army, found himself in Remagen, Germany, thousands of miles from his hometown of Buffalo, New York. At the time, U.S. forces commanded by General Omar Bradley were driving deep into the territory of Nazi Germany, battling the last-ditch resistance of the retreating German forces.

World War II had been raging in Europe since 1939, when the Nazi dictator Adolf Hitler had unleashed his armies on Germany's European neighbors. For a while, Hitler's forces had threatened to engulf the Western world; but after Germany's invasion of the Soviet Union ended in disastrous defeat, the tide began to turn in favor of the Allies: the Soviet Union, Great Britain, France, and the United States. In June 1944, the Allies' massive invasion of German-occupied France began the final bloody chapter of the European conflict. Like so many other young Americans, Spahn had had his life interrupted by the war. In December 1942, a year after the

Warren Spahn as a member of the Boston Braves during the 1942 season. Spahn was just beginning to realize his potential as a left-handed pitching prospect when World War II interrupted his big league career.

United States entered the conflict, he had been drafted by the army and assigned to the combat engineers. Spahn had accepted the turn of events uncomplainingly, knowing that he was only one of millions who were being asked to serve their country in a desperate hour.

Unlike most other recruits, however, Spahn had not walked away from a college classroom or a nine-to-five job in an office or factory. He was, instead, a professional baseball player who had traded in his glove and spikes for a rifle and a steel helmet. Other ballplayers had done the same, many with much greater reputations than Spahn's. Ted Williams of the Boston Red Sox, for example, who had batted a phenomenal .406 in 1941, was training combat pilots for the U.S. Navy, while the Cleveland Indians' Bob Feller, a fireballing right-hander with three 20-win seasons under his belt, was serving as an antiaircraft gunner on the battleship *Alabama*.

Spahn could hardly compare himself to superstars such as Williams and Feller. There had been no headlines in the newspapers when he joined the army, and none of his fellow soldiers had even heard of him. A young left-hander with a history of shoulder trouble, he had spent three years in the Boston Braves minor league system, enjoying only a few brief relief outings in the majors. But baseball people had been thrilled by his potential. "That Warren Spahn can become one of the best pitchers in baseball," Braves manager Casey Stengel had told reporters, "if nothing happens to him."

Stengel had been referring only to Spahn's history of arm trouble. But with the young hurler now enmeshed in some of the fiercest fighting of World War II, his entire future could not have been more uncertain. As the Allied forces advanced toward the German capital of Berlin, the combat engineers were in the front lines, carrying out the unglamorous but crucial task of repairing the roads and bridges wrecked by the retreating Germans.

On March 7, 1945, the U.S. Ninth Armored Division reached the Rhine River, the gateway to the German heartland, at the ancient town of Remagen. German forces, desperately striving to delay the Allied advance, had destroyed all the bridges spanning the Rhine; but in their hasty retreat, they had missed the railway bridge at Remagen. Seizing this unexpected opportunity, the tanks of the Ninth Division rumbled across the river, and five more divisions followed swiftly to establish a bridgehead on the Rhine's eastern bank.

Sergeant Spahn's battalion was assigned the crucial task of maintaining the Remagen bridge while masses of troops, tanks, and trucks poured over it around the clock. Their job was made even more difficult by the determination of the Germans to destroy the bridge at all costs. As the engineers worked to buttress the girders and maintain the roadway, they were subjected to bombardment from German V-2 rockets and narrowly averted a German attempt to demolish the bridge by means of a barge loaded with dynamite.

Ten days after the first crossing, the crippled German air force gathered its forces and launched a sudden assault on Remagen. As the engineers worked on the bridge, German bombers swept over the Rhine and released their deadly cargo. One of the bombs made a direct hit on the bridge. Twenty-five engineers were killed immediately, and many others were seriously wounded. As the army medics rushed to help the casualties, they found Sergeant Spahn with his leg torn up by shrapnel.

Fortunately for Spahn, the army surgeons were able to remove the jagged fragments of steel and save his leg. For his heroism under fire he was awarded a battlefield citation, becoming the only major league player to receive such an honor during World War II. (Bob Feller and his shipmates on the *Alabama* won eight battle stars in the Pacific, but the citations were awarded to the entire crew rather than to individuals.) However, as he lay in a military hospital, slowly recoving from his wounds, Spahn had

U.S. tanks roll over the railway bridge at Remagen, Germany, in March 1945. As one of the combat engineers assigned to maintain the bridge, Spahn suffered a serious leg wound during a German air raid later in the month.

to wonder if he would ever have a genuine major league career. The cards seemed to be stacked against him: first a shoulder injury, now a seriously wounded leg. By the time the war was over and he could return to baseball, he would be at least 25, and he would have gone more than three years without throwing a pitch to a big league hitter. His prospects could hardly have been dimmer.

However, Spahn did not give up on the dreams of baseball glory he had cherished since his youth, and finally things began to go his way. To the fans who grew up watching him exert his mastery over National League hitters during the two decades that followed the war, it seemed incredible that his career had ever been in doubt. Spahn not only made his mark in the major leagues; he went on to rewrite the record books. During the course of 21 seasons, a remarkable feat of durability for a pitcher, Spahn won 363 games—the fifth-highest total in baseball history and the most ever for a left-hander. He seemed to get better as he grew older, throwing two no-hitters after the age of 39 and enjoying a 20-win season, the last of his 13, at the age of 42.

Warren Spahn turned out to be one of baseball's greatest pitchers. But his career also taught one of baseball's most important lessons. With patience, hard work, and a dedication to continue the struggle for excellence, even in the face of seemingly overwhelming odds, all things are possible—in baseball as in every other walk of life.

2

WHO'S ON FIRST?

Warren Edward Spahn was born on April 23, 1921, in Buffalo, New York. Growing up in the late 1920s and early 1930s in Buffalo's blue-collar East End, Spahn saw himself playing in the big leagues one day, as so many youngsters do, but he had no ideas about being a pitcher. His boyhood heroes were the game's top slugging first basemen, Lou Gehrig of the New York Yankees and the Detroit Tigers' Hank Greenberg. Because Buffalo had no major league team, young Warren never got to see either of his idols play. He could only read about their exploits in the newspapers and hear about them on the radio when the Yankees or the Tigers played in the World Series.

However, Buffalo did have a top-notch minor league team, the Buffalo Bisons of the International League. Warren and his father, Ed, made regular trips to Bison Stadium in downtown Buffalo to see the Bisons in action. Warren quickly found a local hero in the slick-fielding Buffalo first-sacker Bill Kelly. After watching Kelly in action, Warren would practice

As a member of Buffalo's South Park High School baseball squad, Spahn led his team to the city championship in 1939 and 1940. After graduation, he signed a major league contract with the Boston Braves.

his moves around first base for hours on end at the crude sandlot diamond near home.

The youngster had been named after Warren G. Harding, the nation's president at the time of his birth. But from an early age the Spahns' firstborn son made it clear that baseball and not politics was his passion. After all, he was growing up in an era when Gehrig's teammate Babe Ruth was the nation's biggest celebrity, drawing an even higher salary during the late 1920s than President Calvin Coolidge, Harding's successor in the White House. ("I had a better year than he did," Ruth quipped when asked about the disparity in pay.) It was a time when every American boy gifted with athletic talent dreamed of being a baseball star and when other sports were merely there to fill the chilly months between baseball seasons.

Warren's baseball dreams were shared and encouraged by his father, who had also once longed for big league stardom himself. Ed Spahn had had the skill and the desire to reach the big leagues, but his prospects were severely hampered by his size; as an adult he stood five feet seven inches and never weighed more than 130 pounds. Never able to rise much beyond the level of sandlot ball as a youth, Ed Spahn eventually came to terms with reality. He found a job as a wallpaper salesman and spent his summer weekends playing third base for the Lake City Athletic Club of Buffalo's semiprofessional Municipal League.

Like many other disappointed athletes, Ed Spahn was soon reenacting his own frustrated athletic ambitions through his son. Before young Warren was much more than six years old he was already spending long hours in the backyard playing catch and receiving valuable instruction from his enthusiastic father. "Everything I've gotten out of baseball," Spahn would later say, "I certainly owe directly to my father." Ed Spahn was justifiably excited about his young son's promise. "I noticed from the earliest days that he could throw with control and he didn't have any jerk in his motion," the elder Spahn later remembered. Building on this natural ability, Ed Spahn constructed a pitcher's mound in the backyard and patiently taught Warren the art of throwing fastballs and, eventually, curveballs. Ed Spahn knew from experience that as a left-hander his son was best suited to play one of two positions—first base or pitcher. Throwing left-handed allows a first baseman to make a quicker peg to second on a potential double play, and lefthanded pitchers are always in demand in the major leagues. Ed Spahn had learned to be practical. "It may be that you won't turn out to be much of a hitter, and then you'll never get anywhere as a first baseman," he often told Warren. "But if you can pitch you don't have to hit for a hill of beans to make the majors."

Every summer afternoon, Warren would await his father's return from work and then spend the twilight hours hurling a baseball into his father's mitt. The primary lesson of pitching was soon drilled into the youngster's head. "You gotta have control," his father would repeat over and over. "Without control you're nothing! That's the secret. Control!" Even at that early stage, no detail of the pitcher's art was too small. Warren learned how to set himself on the pitching rubber, how to take signals and shake them off, how to pitch with men on base. But time

Baseball action at Buffalo's Bison Stadium, in 1932. Growing up in the western New York metropolis, Spahn was a devoted fan of the hometown Bisons.

and again, the basic lesson was how to hit the catcher's target with each and every toss. "He'd stick this big old catcher's glove in a certain place," Warren remembered years later, "and tell me to hit it. If I didn't, I sometimes didn't get any supper."

When Ed Spahn would cart his son off to the ballpark for a weekend Bisons game—often an action-packed doubleheader— there were new joys in store. The senior Spahn had been a sandlot teammate of Bisons first baseman Bill Kelly. Though a strapping six-footer, Kelly had had little success on the major league level: playing a total of 32 games for the Philadelphia Phillies and the Philadelphia Athletics, he had managed only a .179 batting average. In the minor leagues, however, Kelly was a genuine slugger. Because of his father's friendship with Kelly, young Warren was often allowed on the field to shag balls during batting practice and to tag along after his adopted hero. Despite the long hours of pitching lessons back home, Warren was determined to play first base, like his idol. His attachment to Kelly was so intense that he often forgot the names of the other Buffalo players and called them all "Kelly." The amused Bisons returned the compliment by nicknaming their young mascot "Kelly" Spahn.

Seeing that Warren had his heart set on playing first base, Ed Spahn bought his son a new first baseman's mitt for his ninth birthday and even arranged for the youngster to play first base for the Lake City Social Club midget team. Warren's first great baseball thrill came when he graduated to the Lake City amateur senior team at the age of 13—he still weighed only 110 pounds—and thus played in the same infield with his father, who was still patrolling the hot corner for the local nine. "I thought some of [my father's] throws to first were actually going to knock me into the first base bleachers," Spahn later recalled in an interview with Boston sportswriter Harold Kaese.

When 14-year-old Warren Spahn first reported to try out for the baseball team at Buffalo's South Park High School, he fully intended to play first base. But he was still a scrawny youngster, and South Park already had a crack first baseman in burly Bill Benzerman, an all-conference player who had nailed down the position the previous season.

South Park's coach, Joe Shumaker, asked Warren if he could play any other position. Though deeply dejected by the impossibility of his playing first, Warren admitted that he had done some pitching, and the coach offered him a tryout on the mound. After only a few pitches, a delighted Shumaker knew that he had a potential star on his hands. "He already had perfect control," the coach later remembered, "and the local papers thought I was nuts when I was soon saying young Spahn would be another Lefty Grove." (The magnificent Grove, who had gone 31-4 for the Philadelphia Athletics in 1931, was well on his way to 300 career wins and a plaque in the Hall of Fame.) The coach did not have to listen to the sportswriters' jokes for very long. South Park High soon emerged as a baseball juggernaut in Buffalo's high school league, behind the unhittable pitching of young Warren Spahn. As a junior and senior, Spahn led his school team to the Cornell Cup as Buffalo public school champs. He pitched one no-hitter his senior season and missed a second consecutive masterpiece by virtue of a lone scratch single.

Spahn's reputation soon spread beyond Buffalo, and during his senior season, big league

Bill Kelly, shown here with a young fan, spent most of his baseball career with the Buffalo Bisons. Though Spahn was determined to be a first baseman like Kelly, his father urged him to develop his skills as a pitcher.

scouts were flocking to the local high school games to see the touted youngster pitch. The New York Yankees were reportedly interested, but Yankees scouts soon rejected the young prospect because he was too skinny.

One scout who did not turn away was Billy Myers, who was working for the Boston Braves. Despite the youngster's scrawny physique, Meyers felt that he had rarely seen a high school pitcher with such great potential. However, when Myers rushed to the Spahn home to offer a Boston contract, Ed Spahn announced that his son would have to finish school before he could even think about playing professional baseball.

At first, Warren was surprised and disappointed by his father's apparent change in goals. "I don't get it, Pop!" he complained. "Isn't this what we have worked for all these years? What if I get hurt, or they are no longer interested in me next season?" But Ed Spahn knew that life did not always work out the way people wanted it to. "Look at me, son!" he argued. "When I couldn't make it all the way in baseball, I wasn't prepared for anything else." Warren's first baseball teacher had learned more than the art of ballplaying. He was determined that Warren would at least have a high school diploma to fall back on.

The apparent gamble turned out to be a prudent course of action. Myers was willing to wait, and as soon as Warren finished his senior year at South Park High, a Braves contract was ready for him. By later standards, it was not a very big contract. But Warren was happy nonetheless. "If I could pay them money to play I would," he told his mother.

3

CLIMBING THE HILL

Immediately after his high school graduation in the spring of 1940, a confident Warren Spahn proudly reported to the Bradford ballclub of the Pony League. The manager who would guide the youngster in his abbreviated rookie season was a crusty old veteran named Jack Onslow. Onslow carried all the usual superstitions of any hardened baseball old-timer of that period. Thus, when the rookie hurler greeted his new skipper with a request for number 13, which he had worn at South Park High, he was promptly given his first stern pro baseball lesson. "We don't carry no number thirteens around here, kid," Onslow is reported to have jawed at his young pitcher. "A guy's liable to run into enough tough luck around here without any number thirteen on his back."

Onslow's statement soon proved to be prophetic. Little more than a month into the season, Spahn was experimenting with a new overhand curve along the sidelines when he felt something snap deep in his left shoulder. A terrible pain shot down his arm. As Onslow and

Spahn shows his form at the Braves spring training camp in March 1942. Coming off a 19-win season in the minor leagues, Spahn was rated one of the team's top pitching prospects.

the team's trainer rushed to the rookie's side, they could see by the grimace on his face that something was seriously wrong with him. A medical examination confirmed the worst: Spahn had severely torn several tendons in his left shoulder. He was sent home to Buffalo for an extended period of rest, his arm in a sling and his pitching dreams in ruins.

Spahn arrived back in Buffalo crestfallen and dejected. He worried most of all about his father's reaction, which proved to be every bit as gloomy as he had feared. And he fretted about his cloudy baseball future. He had won only 5 and lost 4 in his first 12 outings at Bradford, hardly a way to turn heads in Boston, he thought. It was true that his teammates had failed to support him with good hitting or fielding. His ERA was solid at 2.73, as was his control with 62 strikeouts and only 24 walks in 66 innings pitched. But Spahn wanted to control his own destiny in the Braves organization. A mere two weeks after his injury, the young left-hander was back on the train to Bradford. His arm was still wrapped in a sling, but his mind was bent on a quick comeback.

"I think I'm about ready to pitch again," the desperate youngster told Onslow when he showed up as a surprise visitor, without his sling, in the team clubhouse. This may have been the only time in his career that Spahn failed to use good baseball judgement. Onslow, desperate for some left-handed pitching help for his young and struggling club, was equally over-anxious. So when Spahn insisted that he was ready to throw after only two weeks' rest, Onslow reluctantly gave him the go-ahead.

The experiment was a disaster. The split second the first pitch left Spahn's fingers, he knew he had made a terrible mistake. Another jolt of pain shot through his shoulder, and he dropped to his knees in agony. This time the recovery period would be much longer. Spahn was on the next train home, with strict orders not to exercise or even lift his arm again until the coming spring at the very earliest.

If things had not gone well on the ballfield for the young pitching prospect, they had not exactly been bright on the home front, either. Ed Spahn had replaced his own baseball dreams with more serious adult preoccupations, such as earning a living and raising a family. Eventually, he hoped to live out his frustrated ambition of athletic fame through his son. But when the dream apparently died a second time with Warren's injury, Ed Spahn found the disappointment too much to bear. He fell into a deep depression, and his condition was so serious that he had to be hospitalized.

With his father unable to work and hardly able to even recognize his wife and children, Warren had little time to mope around the house feeling sorry for himself and his own fading baseball prospects. As the oldest son in a family of eight, he was now pressed into service to support his struggling family. Through the remainder of the summer and into the fall and winter, the 19-year-old spent his days working as a baggage checker at the Buffalo railroad terminal. Fortunately, he did not have to do much lifting, and he was able to rest his slow-healing shoulder. At night he would sit long hours by his father's bedside, talking about his plans to take to the diamond the following spring and

Jack Onslow, a former major league catcher, managed Spahn during the pitcher's first season in the minors. The young left-hander performed well for Onslow, but a serious shoulder injury nearly put an end to his baseball career.

renew the shared baseball dreams that had been so unexpectedly interrupted.

Ed Spahn's spirits eventually lifted, just as Warren's shoulder healed with time. By the spring of 1941, the young left-hander found himself back at the Braves preseason training camp in San Antonio, Texas, throwing hard once more and struggling to work the kinks out of a long-inactive pitching arm. Fate had one more trick to play, however, before Spahn's baseball career could get itself back on track. While testing his once-tender shoulder along the sidelines before an exhibition game, he was suddenly struck in the face by a wild throw from one of his teammates. While his badly broken nose did not keep him sidelined for long, the outward effects of the injury were to stay with the young hurler forever. Spahn's nose had always been on the large side, and the accident did nothing to improve its shape. Before long, his teammates were branding him with such memorable nicknames as the Great Profile and Hook. These tags stuck to him through all the years of his big league career.

Spahn pitched a full season for Evansville of the Three-I League in 1941, showing great promise as he led the circuit with 19 wins and a 1.83 ERA. Thus when spring training time rolled around again in March 1942, his slow-starting pitching career finally seemed to have gotten off the ground. Now 20 years old, Spahn impressed the Braves management in spring training and earned a spot on the big league club in Boston. But it was only to be a brief trial. The United States had entered World War II after the Japanese attack on Pearl Harbor in December 1941, and hundreds of thousands of young men—including major league ballplayers—were being drafted into the armed forces. The Braves wanted to see what they could expect from their younger pitchers if the the wartime call-up deprived them of any established hurlers.

After two token relief appearances in the opening weeks of the 1942 season, Spahn was back with the Eastern League farm club in Hartford, Connecticut, destined for another summer of minor league seasoning. If he resented the move, he hardly showed it. Once again he went out and dazzled minor league hitters with his assortment of fastballs and curves, winning 17 games and again posting a sterling mark of less than two earned runs per game.

Toward the end of the season, it was finally time for the ambitious young hurler to get another taste of big league action. Spahn made a brief return with the Braves in September 1942. There was little he or anyone else could do to lift the team at that point, with the Braves occupying seventh place in an eight-team league, 44 games behind the first-place St. Louis Cardinals. But Spahn showed enough to Boston manager Casey Stengel, who asserted that only an injury could prevent the youngster from becoming a star. Spahn's arm stayed healthy, but World War II came very close to putting him on the shelf for good.

Spahn receives encouragement from his fiancée, Lorene Southard, before facing the New York Giants on August 10, 1946. Spahn won the game, and he and Southard were married in a private ceremony on the following day.

4

"PRAY FOR RAIN"

When Warren Spahn was discharged from the army late in the spring of 1946, baseball loomed large in his thoughts, but it was not his only priority. Before shipping out for combat duty in Europe, Spahn had been stationed in Tulsa, Oklahoma. While there he had dated Lorene Southard, an attractive Oklahoman who worked as a secretary for an oil company. The young couple had discussed marriage, but with an uncertain fate awaiting Spahn in the combat zone, they had decided to wait for the end of the war. By the spring of 1946, Spahn had recovered from his leg wound and was safely back in Oklahoma with Southard, ready to resume his personal life and—he hoped—his major league career.

Throughout the winter and into the spring, Southard had received a steady stream of telephone calls from Braves general manager John Quinn, who was eager to know when Spahn was slated to return. Southard did not relish the idea of losing Spahn again, even if it was to baseball rather than military combat. But as long as the Braves still wanted him, there was no way of holding the young pitcher back from another crack at the majors. Less than four hours after reaching Tulsa, he was on another train heading for Pittsburgh, Pennsylvania, where the struggling Braves were playing the Pirates.

On June 10, Spahn walked into the Braves clubhouse at Pittsburgh's Forbes Field and rejoined his teammates. A week later he made his first mound appearance in four years, pitching in relief during a Bunker Hill Day doubleheader back at Braves Field in Boston. After two more brief appearances out of the bullpen, Spahn got his first big league start, gaining a 4–1 victory over the Pirates. Having broken the ice, he went on to win his next four starts.

Spahn finished the season with a respectable if not spectacular 8-5 record and a solid ERA of 2.94. Though the Braves finished 15½ games behind the St. Louis Cardinals, they did reach the first division for the first time in years, finishing fourth by a wide margin. For Braves fans, who had not had a true pitching star to cheer for since the days of Dick Rudolph during the 1910s and early 1920s, Spahn's reappearance was a pure delight.

The fans were excited not so much by Spahn's numbers as by his style on the mound. Once an undersized youngster, Spahn had grown to be six feet tall; at 172 pounds, he was trim, sinewy, and perfectly coordinated. As the veteran Boston sportswriter Al Silverman phrased it, "Watching Spahn for the first time go into his delivery was an aesthetic experience, like seeing a famous painting for the first time. . . . The Spahn windup was the most picturesque, the most graceful, the most beautiful windup I had ever seen from a pitcher."

Spahn had waited a long time to establish

himself in the big leagues, but he was determined not to wait much longer to marry Lorene Southard. As a part of their campaign to get him back on the mound in a hurry, the Braves had promised to foot the bill for a fancy wedding at the end of the season. But Spahn was extremely unhappy during his first weeks on the road, as Southard remained back in Tulsa while he crisscrossed the baseball circuit. After talking things over, Spahn and Southard decided not to wait. When the Braves had an open date in early August, the young couple were married in a private ceremony.

Spahn's abbreviated 1946 season had gained him a footing in the major leagues, and during the following year, he established himself as a top-notch National League hurler. During spring training for the 1947 season, he worked for hours on end with pitching coach Johnny Cooney, perfecting his mechanics and learning a variety of off-speed pitches to go with his fastball and curve. He came out of the gate quickly, winning his first eight starts and missing a ninth win only because of a lucky hit by Johhny Moore of the Cardinals. At the All-Star break, Spahn was the hottest pitcher in baseball, with an 11-3 record. His efforts earned him a berth on the National League All-Star team along with another Braves hurler, Johnny Sain. During the midsummer classic, played at Chicago's Wrigley Field, Spahn pitched the final two innings, holding the American League All-Stars scoreless as the Nationals struggled in vain to overcome a 2–1 deficit.

By the end of the season, Spahn's record stood at 21-10, and his 2.33 ERA led the league. Sain, a tall right-hander from Havana, Arkansas, also posted 21 wins, against 12 losses. Suddenly blessed with the best one-two pitching combination in baseball, the once-lowly Braves shot up to third place with a record of 86-68, finishing only 8 games behind the Dodgers.

Boston had not seen a pitching combo to match Spahn and Sain in several decades, and the local sportswriters searched for catchy phrases to label the new duo. One enthusiastic scribe, pointing out that the Braves duo cleaned up on so many victories, came up with Spick and Spahn, a play on the name of a popular household cleanser. But the phrase that stuck was "Spahn and Sain, and pray for rain!" Aside from the catchy rhyme, there was a great deal of truth in the saying. Spahn and Sain were almost the only two reliable pitchers available to Braves manager Billy Southworth. During the 1947 season, Spahn had started 40 games, and Sain had started 38—nearly 50 percent of the Braves schedule.

Despite the sudden surge of the Braves, Boston still belonged to the Red Sox of the American League: the majority of Bostonians regarded the Braves as the city's "other" team. That began to change in 1948, when the Braves

Spahn and Johnny Sain, one of the finest pitching combinations in baseball history, warm up before a 1948 game at Braves Field in Boston. During the season, the pair combined for 39 wins and led the Braves to their first pennant in 34 years.

shocked the baseball world—and many of their own fans, perhaps—by winning their first pennant in 34 years. The team was paced by the hitting of outfielder Tommy Holmes (.325) and shortstop Alvin Dark (.322), while Spahn and Sain took care of the pitching chores. Sain enjoyed his finest season in the majors, winning 24 games and posting a 2.60 ERA. Spahn's victory total dipped to 15, but he faithfully took the ball every fourth day and kept his team in the ballgame: from a manager's point of view, this kind of consistency matters as much as the number of wins a pitcher chalks up. Spahn's 257 innings pitched placed him third among the league leaders, and his 16 completed games put him in the top five.

The summer of 1948 was an unforgettable campaign for Boston baseball fans. Not only did the Braves vault to the top of the National League: the Red Sox, paced by Ted Williams and Vern Stephens, engaged in a torrid three-way pennant race with the New York Yankees and the Cleveland Indians. Boston and Cleveland finished in a tie, with the hated Yankees 2½ games back. The Boston faithful were anticipating the first "subway series" in the city's history, but the Indians spoiled the party by winning a special one-game playoff on Lou Boudreau's ninth-inning homer.

The Braves themselves were happy enough to be playing anyone in October, but the 1948 World Series was one of ups and downs for both the team and Spahn. The Series began well enough, as the fans at Braves Field were electrified by their team's opening 1–0 victory behind Sain. The game was decided when Braves catcher Phil Masi scored from second base a single, after Bob Feller had apparently picked him off the bag, only to have the umpire miss the call. But in Game 2, the Indians knocked Spahn out of the box in the fifth inning and evened up the Series with a 4–1 victory. Cleveland then took two close games at home, beating Sain and Vern Bickford. With their backs against the wall in Game 5, the Braves exploded for six runs in the seventh inning and won the game 11–5, with Spahn picking up the win after pitching almost six innings in relief.

Back in Boston, however, the Braves' World Series dream came to an end as the Indians eked out a 4–3 win behind Bob Lemon and Gene Bearden. Spahn again came out of the bullpen, pitching the final two innings in relief and allowing the deciding run on three straight singles in the eighth.

After falling short of a world championship in 1948, the Braves settled back into mediocrity, finishing fourth in each of the next three seasons. Johnny Sain also began to decline after his 20-win season in 1950, and the following year he was traded to the Yankees. As the team declined, so did attendance at Braves Field. The Red Sox once again dominated the Boston baseball scene, and few people bothered to show up at Braves games, even when Spahn was pitching.

Spahn did whatever he could to provide a bright spot for Braves fans during the lean years. In 1949, 1950, and 1951, he posted 21, 21, and 22 wins, pitching 290 or more innings each season. The pitcher who had once appeared frail and injury-prone was proving to be an iron man on the mound.

In 1952, however, everything came apart, both for Spahn and the Braves. Spahn won only 14 games while losing 19, the worst season he would ever suffer through as a full-time starting

Spahn delivers a pitch to Cleveland's Dale Mitchell during Game 2 of the 1948 World Series. Though he was charged with the loss in the game, Spahn came back in Game 5 with six innings of strong relief work, emerging as the winning pitcher in an 11–5 triumph.

pitcher. Under managers Tommy Holmes and Charlie Grimm, the Braves managed a mere 64 wins and finished a distant seventh, trailed only by the even more dismal Pittsburgh Pirates. As bad as the team was, attendance was even worse. During the entire 77-game home schedule, only 280,000 paying customers showed up at Braves Field, an average of slightly more than 3,600 per game.

When Boston sportswriter John Gillooly called the Braves "the worst franchise in baseball history," he may have been exaggerating—but he was certainly expressing the sentiments of Boston baseball fans.

5

BASEBALL'S NEW HOMETOWN

Spahn delivers a curve ball during a spring training game in March 1954. During the previous season, the Braves' first in Milwaukee, Spahn had posted a 23-7 record, adding to his stature as one of the game's best pitchers.

By the end of the dreadful 1952 season, it should have come as no surprise when the Boston Braves management proposed to do what no team had done for nearly half a century of modern major league play. After watching his team play the season in a virtually empty ball-park, owner Lou Perini announced that he was going to change the baseball map for the first time since 1903 by moving his team from Boston to the baseball-hungry midwestern city of Milwaukee, Wisconsin.

Despite the dilemma the Braves faced in Boston, Perini's decision sent shock waves through the baseball world. Most fans had never witnessed the relocation of a franchise and had not even imagined such an event. Many feared that one of the basic foundations of the game—the almost sacred bond between a city and its baseball team (or teams)—was being destroyed, and the numerous franchise moves that have occurred since 1952 prove that these fears were not unfounded.

In Milwaukee, however, no one was worried about the foundations of the game or feeling sorry for the citizens of Boston. The wild enthusiasm that surrounded the Braves' first seasons in the Midwest has never been matched in the nation's baseball history. Few cities have ever poured their emotions into baseball the way Milwaukee did in the mid-1950s, and no community apart from Brooklyn has ever taken its team so much to heart.

When the Braves arrived in Milwaukee from spring training on April 8, 1953, more than 12,000 screaming, sign-waving fans were at the station to greet them. A throng of 60,000 filled the downtown streets for a welcoming parade. The following afternoon, 10,000 people turned out in a driving rainstorm, hoping to see an exhibition game between the Braves and Red Sox, but the game was called because of the weather. A week later, an overflow crowd of 34,357 filled County Stadium for the Braves home opener against the Cincinnati Reds. The sale of standing-room tickets alone was greater than the total ticket sale for the Braves home opener in Boston the year before.

More than 1.8 million fans poured through the County Stadium turnstiles during the Braves' first season in Milwaukee, a new league attendance record that smashed the earlier standard set by the Dodgers in 1947. The team that had been so dreadful in Boston seemed to come alive in response to their new fans. They improved their won-lost record in 1953 by a remarkable 28 games and climbed from seventh to second.

The revitalized Braves developed an impressive new cast of characters, topped by Henry "Hank" Aaron, who broke in during the 1954 season, and Eddie Mathews, who had played his first season with the club in Boston in 1952. During their 13 years as teammates, Aaron and Mathews were to hit more home runs than any duo since Babe Ruth and Lou Gehrig.

The Braves also possessed important role players. Johnny Logan proved to be a scrappy shortstop with quick hands and a solid bat, leading the league in doubles in 1957. Burly first baseman Joe Adcock was one of the premier sluggers of his era and stood 20th on the all-time home run list at the end of his career. Billy Bruton, a swift center fielder, led the league in stolen bases during his first three seasons with the Braves. Switch-hitting second baseman Red Schoendienst, who joined the team in 1957 after a standout career with the Cardinals, added the experience and confidence the Braves needed to become champions.

Ultimately, pitching is the crucial factor in the success or failure of a team, and no single individual was more important in the resurgence of the Braves than Warren Spahn. During the Braves' first season in Milwaukee, Spahn led the league with 23 wins (against 7 losses) and a splendid 2.10 ERA, and he followed up with

Braves third baseman Eddie Mathews cracks a home run during the 1959 All-Star Game in Pittsburgh's Forbes Field. When they added sluggers such as Mathews, Hank Aaron, and Joe Adcock to their lineup during the early 1950s, the Braves began their climb from doormats to contenders.

another 20-win season in 1954. In 1955, he dropped to 17-14, but the following year he was back in form, turning in the first of six consecutive 20-win seasons.

The 1956 season, in which Spahn went 20-11 with a 2.78 ERA, was the first year of the Cy Young Award, created to honor baseball's best pitcher. (In 1967, the award was split to honor one pitcher in each league.) Spahn was a leading candidate, along with teammate Lew Burdette, the Indians' Bob Lemon, and Whitey Ford of the Yankees, among others. In the last weeks of the season, Brooklyn's Don Newcombe pulled away from the field, finishing with 27 wins and easily capturing the prestigious award.

The Cy Young Award meant less to Spahn than another crack at the World Series. He was deeply troubled by the way the Braves had stumbled in the 1956 pennant race. After leading the league through the first 126 games of the season, the Braves had begun to falter in the stretch, while the Dodgers, sparked by Newcombe, went on a hot streak. Entering the final weekend of the season, the Braves needed to sweep their three-game series with the Cardinals in order to capture the pennant. They won the first game and seemed a good bet to win the second with Spahn, the ace of the staff, matched up against a journeyman pitcher named Herm Wehmeier, who had been bouncing around the league for several years.

Spahn more than lived up to his billing, pitching no-hit ball for six innings and enjoying a 1–0 lead on the strength of a home run by Bill Bruton. But Wehmeier turned out to be equally effective, holding the Braves to a single run and thus allowing the Cardinals to tie the game in

the late innings. Both pitchers toiled into the 12th, and then the game got away from the Braves. In the bottom half of the inning, Stan Musial lifted a soft fly to right that should have been an easy out but somehow dropped between the outfielders for a double. Spahn then walked Ken Boyer intentionally to set up a double play. The strategy appeared to have worked when the Cardinals' Rip Repulski lashed a one-hopper toward Mathews at third—a tailor-made double-play ball. But fate was not with the Braves and Spahn that night. The ball took a bad hop and caromed off Mathews's knee, allowing Musial to score the winning run.

As he walked to the Braves dugout with his head down, Spahn wept, reportedly for the first time in his life. Even the Cardinals took little pleasure in the outcome. "He's just the greatest pitcher in baseball, that's all," Wehmeier said in the victors' clubhouse. "For the first time in my life I actually feel sorry for the man who pitched against me."

Spahn stares dejectedly into his locker after losing a 12-inning battle against the St. Louis Cardinals on the last weekend of the 1956 season. Though Spahn had enjoyed another solid 20-win campaign, he was deeply disappointed by his team's failure to capture the National League pennant.

PITCHING IN THE CLUTCH

In 1957, the Braves bounced back from their late-season nosedive the previous year and finally replaced the Dodgers at the top of the National League, winning the pennant by eight games. Spahn had waited a decade to get back into the World Series, and no one on the Braves team was likely to enjoy the competition more. As it turned out, the epic battle between the Braves and the American League champion New York Yankees was destined to be a gut-wrenching experience for everyone involved.

When Braves manager Fred Haney picked Spahn to start the opening game in New York's Yankee Stadium, the star hurler was naturally thrilled, but he also felt the responsibility that was being placed on his shoulders. "The one man who has the biggest load to carry is the pitcher who has been named to open the Series," he later reflected. "There's a big psychological advantage in winning the first game. Your reasoning then is that you have forced the other team to beat you in four of the next six games—a .667 pace. That's a pretty good percentage even in the regular season when you're playing second division teams. It's much tougher against a league champion."

Spahn pitched well in the Series opener, but his mound opponent, lefty Whitey Ford, pitched even better. While Ford was holding the Braves to a single run, the Yankees caught up to Spahn in the sixth: after Andy Carey drove in the New Yorkers' second run with a one-out single, Spahn was lifted in favor of reliever Ernie Johnson. The Yankees went on to post a 3–1 victory, and Spahn was charged with the loss. The Braves came back to win Game 2 behind Lew Burdette, breaking through for four runs, and the Braves' ability to score some runs for the right-hander was an omen of things to come. Burdette went on to win two more games in the Series, pitching a full 27 innings without relief and posting a nearly flawless 0.67 ERA. Turning in one of the great individual performances in World Series history, Burdette was the unanimous choice as the most valuable player of the 1957 Series, an honor that many had predicted would belong to Spahn.

Though Burdette's heroics captured the attention of the baseball world, Spahn did have a crucial role to play in the unfolding drama of the Series when he took the mound at County Stadium to start Game 4. The Yankees had won Game 3 behind Bob Turley and Don Larsen, and it was up to Spahn to prevent the Bronx Bombers from taking a commanding 3–1 lead in the Series.

Although he had felt faint with the flu on the eve of the game, Spahn pitched masterfully through eight innings and entered the ninth with a 4–1 lead. He retired the first two batters, and then, when he was only one out away from

a neat six-hit triumph, disaster struck. Gil McDougald and Yogi Berra reached Spahn for base hits, and Yankees catcher Elston Howard stepped up to the plate and blasted a game-tying home run.

In the 10th inning, Spahn weakened still further, as Tony Kubek singled and scored on Hank Bauer's triple. Spahn got out of the inning without further damage, but Milwaukee's dream of a world championship appeared to be fading rapidly. In the bottom of the 10th, however, the tide turned again. Milwaukee's Nippy Jones was

Braves catcher Del Crandall, manager Fred Haney, and second baseman Red Schoendienst confer with Spahn during Game 1 of the 1957 World Series. Spahn allowed only two runs in six innings of work, but he was tagged with the loss as the Yankees went on to a 3–1 victory.

awarded first base after being hit by a pitch; Johnny Logan doubled him home, and Eddie Mathews sent the crowd and the entire city of Milwaukee into a joyous frenzy with his game-winning homer. Fred Haney was rewarded for sticking with his veteran pitcher—Spahn had pitched more skillful games, but he had never turned in a gutsier performance under so much pressure.

Spahn had saved the day for his team, and he might still have ended as the hero of the Series except for another quirk of fate. Even though Burdette won Game 5 with a masterful seven-hit shutout, Spahn was Haney's choice to start Game 7 after the Yankees came back to even the Series with a 3–2 win in Game 6. But on the eve of what could have been his greatest personal triumph, Spahn was flat on his back in a New York hotel room, felled by the flu. There was no way he could take the mound at Yankee Stadium the following afternoon. Burdette was pressed into service with only two days' rest and performed as brilliantly as he had in his previous outings, pitching his second consecutive shutout. As the victorious Braves mobbed Burdette on the mound, the ailing Spahn sat alone in the clubhouse, watching on television.

During the off-season, Spahn had much to celebrate. He was a world champion at last, and his contribution to Milwaukee's pennant drive (21 wins and a 2.69 ERA) was fully recognized by the nation's baseball writers, who awarded him the 1957 Cy Young Award. When the Braves roared back to repeat as National League champions in 1958, Spahn was again at the forefront, leading the league with 22 victories, 290 innings, and 23 complete games.

Best of all, he was getting another crack at the Yankees in the World Series. Matched once again with rival southpaw Whitey Ford in the opener, Spahn hurled his second straight 10-inning Series victory, as the Braves won a 4–3 squeaker on consecutive singles by Joe Adcock, Del Crandall, and Billy Bruton. The win was also a present for Spahn's son Greg, who was celebrating his 10th birthday.

Milwaukee won Game 2 behind Burdette and then took a 3–1 lead in the Series when Spahn came back in Game 4 with a sparkling two-hit, 3–0 shutout, only the 11th two-hitter in more than 50 years of Series play.

Just when it seemed that the once-invincible Yankees were losing their magic, they came charging back from the brink of defeat. They won Game 5 behind Bob Turley and sent Whitey Ford to the mound once again to oppose Spahn in Game 6. This time the usually reliable Ford lasted only an inning, while Spahn pitched into the 10th for the third time in two years. In this extra-inning drama, however, the outcome was not to be a happy one for Spahn and the Braves.

Though the Braves had knocked Ford out of the game with a flurry of hits, they had only been able to score twice, and they nursed a 2–1 lead into the sixth inning. At that point, Fred Haney put Bruton into the game for added defense in center field. As luck would have it, Bruton promptly committed an error that allowed Mickey Mantle to reach third base. Yogi Berra contributed a sacrifice fly, and the game was tied. The teams played on into the 10th, and finally the 37-year-old Spahn ran out of gas. He was tagged for two runs, as Gil McDougald hit a solo home run and Elston Howard, Berra, and

Two of baseball's all-time great left-handers, Spahn and Whitey Ford pose for photographers before hooking up in Game 4 of the 1957 World Series. Ford had pitched the Yankees to victory in Game 1, but this time Spahn and the Braves prevailed with a 4–3 win in 10 innings.

Moose Skowron followed with singles. The Braves came back with a run in the bottom of the 10th, but Bob Turley came out of the bullpen to get the final out, and the Yankees had a 4–3 victory. The tide had turned, and the New Yorkers also captured Game 7 by a 6–2 score before a disheartened throng in Milwaukee.

Spahn's experience in October had been marked by triumphs and disappointments, but his combined record over three Series was certainly creditable: 4 wins, 3 losses, a 3.07 ERA, 47 strikeouts, and only 13 walks in 56 innings pitched. As it turned out, Game 6 of the 1958 Series was to be his last shot at postseason glory. No one could have been blamed for assuming that the 37-year-old veteran was about to enter the downside of an admirable career. However, Spahn soon showed that he had plenty of wins left in his ageless left arm.

NUMBER ONE
SOUTHPAW

The Milwaukee Braves were the toast of the baseball world after their dramatic Series triumph in 1957, but they were also fated to enjoy one of the shortest life spans in modern baseball history. The trouble began when their performance on the field declined steeply during the 1961 and 1962 seasons. Only Hank Aaron and Eddie Mathews continued to hit with authority, and only Warren Spahn remained a consistent winner on a crumbling pitching staff. Before long, the once-delirious Milwaukee fans began to desert the lackluster team, just as another group of Braves fans had done only a decade earlier in Boston. By 1965, Milwaukee's joyous love affair with the Braves was over, and owner Lou Perini was again searching for a new market. This time, when the Braves packed their bags and hit the road, they broke into uncharted territory for major league baseball—the booming city of Atlanta, Georgia.

If the glory days were largely over for the Milwaukee franchise by the late 1950s, Spahn rolled on as though nothing had changed. With remarkable consistency, he won 21 games in 1959, 21 in 1960, and 21 in 1961. He also came up with a few surprises, pitching a pair of no-hitters. The first was a 4–0 whitewash of the Phillies on September 16, 1960, before a sparse gathering of barely 6,000 fans in chilly County Stadium. Twice before, in 1951 and 1953, Spahn had been robbed of a no-hitter by a fluke hit, but this time there was no stopping him. He mowed down the Phillies, allowing a mere 2 walks while striking out 15 batters, a club record and his own personal high for a nine-inning game. The win made Spahn a 20-game winner for the 11th time and the 5th season in a row. Asked to sum up his no-hit performance, Spahn was typically modest. "I threw more fastballs than I usually do and it was getting them out," Spahn remarked. If he had been inclined to boast, he might have pointed out that only 34 of the 105 pitches he threw that night were outside the strike zone.

After 15 seasons, Spahn seemed to have discovered the formula for pitching no-hitters. He had finished with one in 1960, and the 1961 campaign had barely begun when he pitched another, a 1–0 thriller against the San Francisco Giants on April 28. Again the setting was County Stadium, and this time the opposition was tougher. The Giants lineup contained such fearsome hitters as Willie Mays, Willie McCovey, Felipe Alou, and Orlando Cepeda, but on this particular night, they could do nothing with Spahn. Again, he walked only two opposing batters, and both were erased by double plays, so that Spahn faced only the minimum 27 batters—a classic no-hitter.

"You ask me, I say he was not fast," Mays commented after the game. "But he was all pitcher, with amazing control. He kept the hitters off balance with his changing speeds and he never put the ball where you could get much bat on it." Almost 30 years after those twilight practice sessions on the backyard diamond in Buffalo, when he had thrown endless fastballs and curves into his father's mitt, Spahn was still proving to the world that he had learned his lessons well.

Later in the 1961 season, on August 11, Spahn achieved every pitcher's most cherished milestone when he defeated the Chicago Cubs for his 300th career win. Spahn was 40 years old, a time when even the greatest pitchers are usually just holding on, struggling to reach 300 wins or some other cherished goal before leaving the game for good. Spahn, by contrast, was still as good a starting pitcher as any in baseball. After pitching 262 innings and winning 21 games in 1961, he fell off slightly in the following year, finishing with a mark of 18-14. But in 1963 he came back to post his best won-lost record in 10 years, 23-7, with a league-leading 22 complete games. Only the phenomenal pitching of the Dodgers' Sandy Koufax, who went 25-5 with a 1.88 ERA and 306 strikeouts, prevented Spahn from winning the Cy Young Award at the age of 42.

Coming into the 1964 season, Spahn appeared capable of pitching forever. However, after nearly 5,000 innings of work in the big leagues, his 43-year-old body finally rebelled. Slowed by a variety of injuries, Spahn had only 25 starts in 1964 and often found himself relegated to the bullpen. He ended the season with a 6-13 record and a dismal 5.29 ERA. During the winter, Spahn had to confront one of the harshest facts of life in professional sports: the

Spahn demonstrates his pitching technique for teammates on the Mexico City Tigers during January 1966. Now 45 years old, Spahn was playing winter ball in Mexico in the vain hope that a major league team would sign him for the upcoming season.

absence of any true loyalty between club owners and their players.

Spahn had enjoyed 20 great seasons with the Braves, but as far as the Milwaukee management was concerned, he was no longer of any use. Shortly after the end of the season, the Braves sold the best pitcher in their history to the hapless New York Mets, who had finished their third summer of big league play with a record of 53-109. New York's sophisticated baseball fans had grudgingly admired Spahn over the course of two decades as he worked his magic against the hometown Dodgers and Giants, and they treated him with the respect and affection due a future Hall of Famer. But nothing could compensate Spahn for his rejection by the Braves and the decline of his pitching skills. He suffered through half a season with the cellar-dwelling Mets, laboring unhappily as both a relief pitcher and a bullpen coach; after the team released him in midseason, he was eventually signed by the contending San Francisco Giants, who were looking for extra pitching down the stretch.

On September 12, 1965, Spahn won his final major league game, a narrow triumph over the Chicago Cubs in the second game of a doubleheader. The victory was his 363rd, a record for left-handers. In the history of baseball only four men had ever won more games: Walter Johnson and Cy Young in the American League, and Christy Mathewson and Grover Cleveland Alexander in the senior circuit. As one sportswriter jokingly put it, this was about the same as finishing right behind Newton and Einstein on a high school physics exam.

Despite his 7-16 record in 1965, Spahn was convinced that he could still pitch effectively in the major leagues. Even at the age of 44, he had turned in 197 innings of work. Always a fiery competitor, Spahn pitched several games in the Mexican League during the winter, hoping to impress major league scouts. When no major league club expressed interest in signing him for the 1966 season, he did not take it kindly. "I didn't quit baseball," the proud left-hander complained, "but it quit me!"

Spahn became eligible for the Hall of Fame in 1970, and for some strange reason the baseball

Flanked by former manager Casey Stengel and Vera Clemente, the widow of fellow inductee Roberto Clemente, Spahn waves to well-wishers during his induction into the Baseball Hall of Fame. With 363 victories, Spahn ranks as the number one left-hander in baseball history.

writers waited three years before voting him in. There was one compensation for the delay. When Spahn was enshrined in Cooperstown in 1973, his fellow inductees were two great players he had often pitched against: the New York Giants' Monte Irvin and Pittsburgh's Roberto Clemente, who had died in a plane crash the previous winter while on a mission to aid earthquake victims in Guatemala.

When assessing Spahn's remarkable career, many observers felt that he could have handily won 400 games, if not for the years he lost to

military service. But Spahn himself was always philosophical about this matter. "I matured a lot in those three years in the army," he said, "and was therefore a lot more able to handle major league hitters when I broke in at 25 than I could have at 22. And if I had not had that maturity, perhaps I never would have pitched until I was almost 45." In Spahn's own view, three seasons lost at the outset of his career were more than repaid by the priceless experiences that marked his final summers on the hill.

Spahn's even-keeled assessment of his career showed the same stable temperament and supreme self-confidence that had always marked his big league pitching style. He would never be the one to look for excuses. But then again, as the winningest left-hander of all time, he never needed anything but a baseball and a mound to pitch from.

CHRONOLOGY

1921	Born in Buffalo, New York, on April 23
1940	Signs professional contract with Boston Braves and pitches 12 games for Bradford in the Pony League before suffering severe shoulder injury
1941	Leads Three-I League with 19 wins while pitching for Evansville
1942	Makes first major league appearance with Boston Braves
1943–45	Serves as staff sergeant in U.S. Army during World War II; suffers serious leg wound and is decorated for bravery in action
1946	Returns from military service and earns spot as regular pitcher with Braves, winning eight games; marries Lorene Southard
1947	Leads National League in ERA while posting first 20-victory season
1948	Pitches in World Series against the Cleveland Indians and wins Game 5 in relief
1952	Leads the National League in strikeouts for the fourth straight year
1953	Braves move from Boston to Milwaukee in first major league franchise shift in half a century; Spahn posts a 23-7 record and earns his third National League ERA title
1957	Pitches 41st career shutout, establishing a new record for National League left-handers; posts eighth 20-win season, the most for any National League left-hander; captures Young Award as baseball's best pitcher; earns extra-inning victory in Game 4 as Braves defeat the Yankees in World Series
1958	Records third straight 20-win season; wins two of three starts in World Series, though Braves lose to Yankees
1960	Hurls first no-hitter of big league career, a 4–0 blanking of Philadelphia Phillies
1961	Pitches second no-hitter with 1–0 win over San Francisco Giants; wins 300th career game; enjoys sixth consecutive 20-win season
1963	Finishes season with 23-7 record, recording 20 victories for the 13th time, a record for left-handers
1964	In final season for Braves, hits 35th career home run, a record for pitchers in the National League; Braves sell Spahn to New York Mets during off-season
1965	Spahn splits season between Mets and San Francisco Giants
1966	Pitches several games in Mexican League before retiring from baseball
1973	Inducted into the Baseball Hall of Fame in Cooperstown, New York

WARREN EDWARD SPAHN

BOSTON N.L., MILWAUKEE N.L.,
NEW YORK N.L., SAN FRANCISCO N.L.,
1942-1965
BECAME FIFTH BIGGEST WINNER IN MAJORS'
HISTORY WITH 363 VICTORIES. MOST
VICTORIES FOR A LEFT-HANDER. WON 20
OR MORE GAMES 13 SEASONS, SIX IN A ROW.
SET ALL-TIME RECORDS FOR YEARS LEADING
LEAGUE IN VICTORIES (8) AND COMPLETE
GAMES (9). ALSO N.L. CAREER HIGHS WITH
665 GAMES STARTED; 5,264 INNINGS;
2,853 STRIKEOUTS. PITCHED NO-HITTER
IN 1960, ANOTHER IN 1961.

MAJOR LEAGUE STATISTICS

BOSTON BRAVES, MILWAUKEE BRAVES, NEW YORK METS, SAN FRANCISCO GIANTS

YEAR	TEAM	W	L	PCT	ERA	G	GS	CG	IP	H	BB	SO	SHo
1942	BOS N	0	0	-	5.74	4	2	1	15.2	25	11	7	0
1946		8	5	.615	2.94	24	16	8	125.2	107	36	67	0
1947		21	10	.677	2.33	40	35	22	289.2	245	84	123	7
1948		15	12	.556	3.71	36	35	16	257	237	77	114	3
1949		21	14	.600	3.07	38	38	25	302.1	283	86	151	4
1950		21	17	.553	3.16	41	39	25	293	248	111	191	1
1951		22	14	.611	2.98	39	36	26	310.2	278	109	164	7
1952		14	19	.424	2.98	40	35	19	290	263	73	183	5
1953	MIL N	23	7	.767	2.10	35	32	24	265.2	211	70	148	5
1954		21	12	.636	3.14	39	34	23	283.1	262	86	136	1
1955		17	14	.548	3.26	39	32	16	245.2	249	65	110	1
1956		20	11	.645	2.78	39	35	20	281.1	249	52	128	3
1957		21	11	.656	2.69	39	35	18	271	241	78	111	4
1958		22	11	.667	3.07	38	36	23	290	257	76	150	2
1959		21	15	.583	2.96	40	36	21	292	282	70	143	4
1960		21	10	.677	3.50	40	33	18	267.2	254	74	154	4
1961		21	13	.618	3.02	38	34	21	262.2	236	64	115	4
1962		18	14	.563	3.04	34	34	22	269.1	248	55	118	0
1963		23	7	.767	2.60	33	33	22	259.2	241	49	102	7
1964		6	13	.316	5.29	38	25	4	173.2	204	52	78	1
1965	2 teams	NY N (20G 4-12)			SF N (16G 3-4)								
total		7	16	.304	4.01	36	30	8	197.2	210	56	90	0
Totals		363	245	.597	3.09	750	665	382	5243.2	4830	1434	2583	63
World Series													
Totals 3 yrs.		4	3	.571	3.05	8	6	3	56	47	13	32	1
All-Star Games													
Totals 7yrs.		1	0	1.000	3.21	7	3	0	14	17	5	10	0

FURTHER READING

Broeg, Bob. "Warren Spahn." In *Super Stars of Baseball.* St. Louis: Sporting News, 1971.

Brosnan, Jim. "Warren Spahn." In *Great Baseball Pitchers.* New York: Random House, 1965.

Buege, Bob. *The Milwaukee Braves: A Baseball Eulogy.* Milwaukee: Douglas American Sports Publications, 1988.

Daley, Arthur. "Warren Spahn." In *All the Home Run Kings.* New York: Putnam, 1972.

Hirshberg, Al. "Milwaukee's Mr. Strikeout." *Sport,* August 15, 1953.

Kahn, Roger. "The Art of Warren Spahn." *Sport,* June 25, 1958.

Larson, Lloyd. "Spahn's Greatness Grows with the Years." *Baseball Digest,* February 19, 1970.

Molter, Harry. "Warren Spahn." In *Famous American Athletes of Today.* 13th series. New York: Page, 1953.

Reichler, Joseph L. "Is Warren Spahn the Best Ever?" *Sport,* May 1964.

Shapiro, Milton J. *The Warren Spahn Story.* New York: Julian Messner, 1958.

———. "Warren Spahn." In *Baseball's Greatest Pitchers.* New York: Julian Messner, 1969.

Silverman, Al. *Warren Spahn, Immortal Southpaw.* New York: Bartholomew House, 1961.

———. "Warren Spahn." In *More Sports Titans of the 20th Century.* New York: Putnam, 1969.

INDEX

URE CREDITS

Wide World Photos: pp. 2, 35, 36; The *Buffalo News,* file photo: p. 14; National Baseball Library, Cooperstown,
pp. 25, 60; Courtesy Joseph M. Overfield, Tonawanda, NY: pp. 18, 20; UPI/Bettmann: pp. 8, 12, 22, 28–29, 32,
41, 42, 45, 48, 50, 54, 56, 58.

PETER C. BJARKMAN, also known as "Doctor Baseball," is the author of more than 20 baseball biographies and history books, including the two-volume *Encyclopedia of Major League Baseball Team Histories*, *The Baseball Scrapbook*, and *Baseball & the Game of Life: Stories for the Thinking Fan*. In addition, he has written *The History of the NBA* and the *Encyclopedia of Pro Basketball Team Histories*. Dr. Bjarkman has also taught English and linguistics at Purdue University and the University of Colorado and currently lives in Lafayette, Indiana, with his wife, Dr. Ronnie Wilbur, a college professor. He is the author of *Roberto Clemente, Duke Snider*, and *Ernie Banks* in the Chelsea House BASEBALL LEGENDS series.

JIM MURRAY, veteran sports columnist of the *Los Angeles Times*, is one of America's most acclaimed writers. He has been named "America's Best Sportswriter" by the National Association of Sportscasters and Sportswriters 14 times, was awarded the Red Smith Award, and was twice winner of the National Headliner Award. In addition, he was awarded the J. G. Taylor Spink Award in 1987 for "meritorious contributions to baseball writing." With this award came his 1988 induction into the National Baseball Hall of Fame in Cooperstown, New York. In 1990, Jim Murray was awarded the Pulitzer Prize for Commentary.

EARL WEAVER is the winningest manager in the Baltimore Orioles' history by a wide margin. He compiled 1,480 victories in his 17 years at the helm. After managing eight different minor league teams, he was given the chance to lead the Orioles in 1968. Under his leadership the Orioles finished lower than second place in the American League East only four times in 17 years. One of only 12 managers in big league history to have managed in four or more World Series, Earl was named Manager of the Year in 1979. The popular Weaver had his number 5 retired in 1982, joining Brooks Robinson, Frank Robinson, and Jim Palmer, whose numbers were retired previously. Earl Weaver continues his association with the professional baseball scene by writing, broadcasting, and coaching.